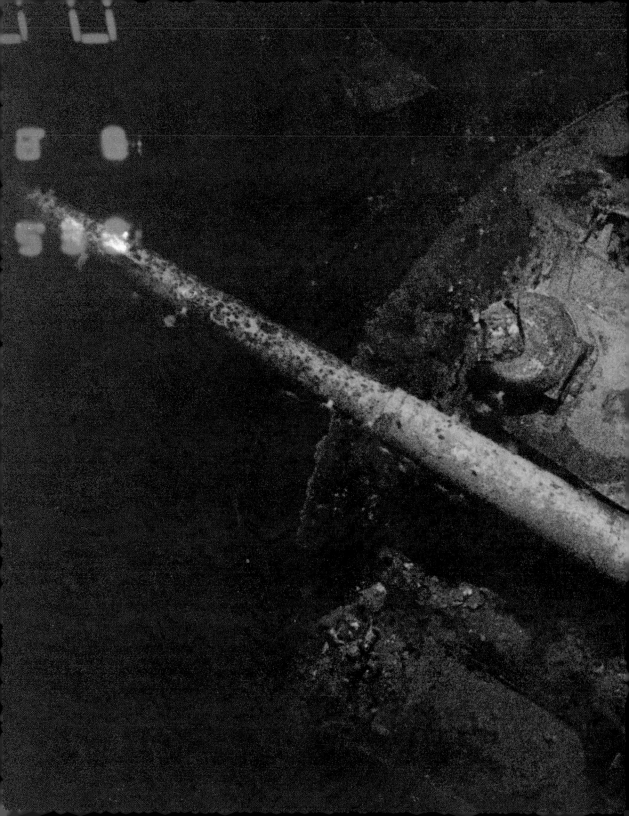

Bismarck!

BY FRANK SLOAN

A FIRST BOOK
FRANKLIN WATTS
NEW YORK/LONDON/TORONTO/SYDNEY/1991

Cover photographs courtesy of AP/Wide World Photos and U.S. Naval Institute (inset)

Photographs courtesy of: AP/Wide World Photos: pp. 2, 3, 10, 14, 26, 27, 46, 54; U.S. Naval Institute: pp. 17, 18; Imperial War Museum: pp. 21, 22, 23, 32, 38, 49; UPI/Bettmann Newsphotos: p. 47; Woods Hole Oceanographic Institution: p. 52.

Library of Congress Cataloging-in-Publication Data

Sloan, Frank.
Bismarck! / by Frank Sloan.
p.   cm. — (A First book)
Includes bibliographical references and index.
Summary: Describes the campaign in World War II to sink the Bismarck and the efforts to salvage its remains.
ISBN 0-531-20002-7
1. Bismarck (Battleship)—Juvenile literature.   2. World War, 1939–1945—Naval operations, British—Juvenile literature.   3. World War, 1939–1945—Naval operations, German—Juvenile literature.
[1. Bismarck (Battleship)   2. World War, 1939–1945—Naval operations, British.   3. World War, 1939–1945—Naval operations, German.]   I. Title.   II. Series.
D772.B5S56   1991
940.54'5941—dc20   90-47858
                                                                            CIP
                                                                            AC

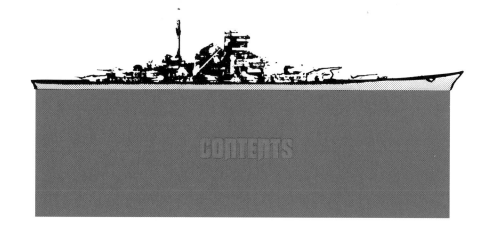

CONTENTS

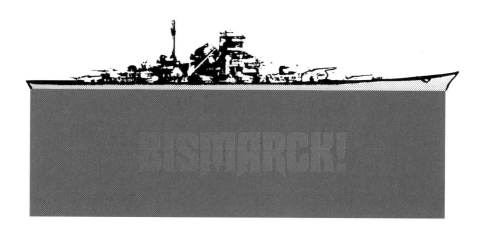

BISMARCK!

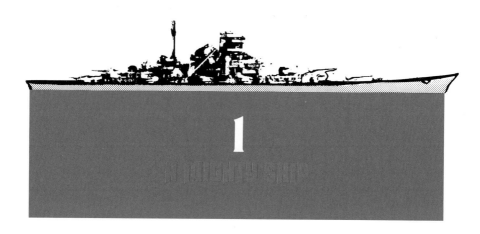

1

Swastika! The dreaded symbol of Nazi Germany. There was no question about it. It could be seen, not clearly. But it was there, right across the top of the ship's deck.

The team of underwater technicians had been scouring the sea for weeks. The scientists had been there the summer before, just off the coast of France. But they had failed to find any trace of what they were looking for. For weeks they had searched for a ship: the great German battleship *Bismarck*. On their TV monitors, the scientists had seen pieces of wreckage, but the debris turned out to be from a nineteenth-century schooner.

Down below, just above the ocean bottom, their sledlike submersible bumped along. The submersible

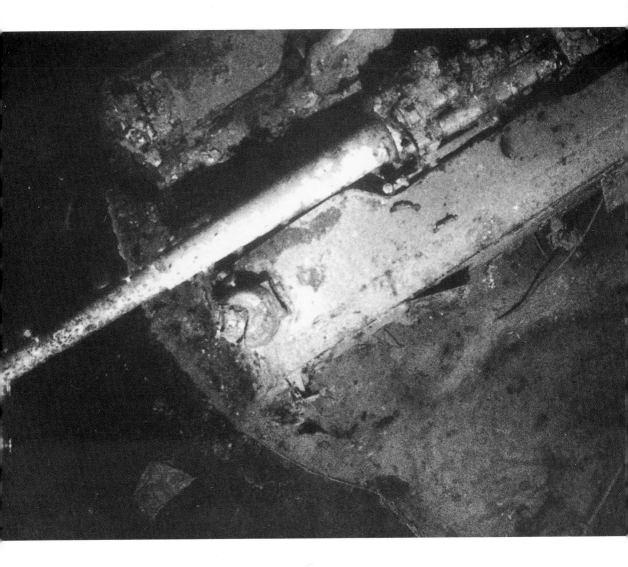

One of the Bismarck's *antiaircraft guns sits on the bottom of the Atlantic in a photo taken by the submersible* Argo.

was taking pictures of every possible bit of the ocean floor. Everyone hoped the cameras would find wreckage from the battleship. But nothing seemed to belong to the *Bismarck*.

Then, suddenly, on June 8, 1989, the search was over.

Step back in time, some fifty years, to September 1939. Adolf Hitler's Nazi troops had just marched across the Polish border and World War II began in Europe. Poland's neighbor to the south, Czechoslovakia, had already fallen to Germany. The strength of Hitler's army grew and grew.

In the spring of 1940, Denmark gave up and let Hitler's troops overrun the country. At the same time Germany conquered Norway. And then, perhaps saddest of all, France fell to Hitler and was occupied by the Germans. Suddenly much of Europe, from north to south, was in German hands. When France fell to Germany, several key cities on France's Atlantic Ocean coast became available to the German navy. Ports such as Brest and St.-Nazaire became home to Nazi U-boats, and submarine bases were quickly set up.

Within a few short months Hitler had gained control of most of Western Europe. But there was one holdout, and it was an important one. Hitler desperately wanted to conquer Great Britain so that the

Germans would be even closer to the Atlantic Ocean. This would let them monitor all shipping in and out of Europe. But the British fiercely resisted Hitler's attempts to conquer them.

Already German U-boats had done a good job of sinking British ships. The number of British ships sunk was so large that the figures were no longer made public. Every effort was made to keep British morale high. At this time the United States had not yet entered the war. England was on its own.

The German navy had been building new and stronger warships. They were needed to patrol the Atlantic and drive all but German ships from the ocean.

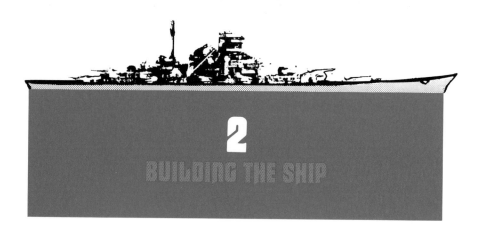

The *Bismarck* was exactly the kind of ship that was needed to upset British shipping and morale. The great ship was a symbol of Germany's greatness and power. After Germany's defeat in World War I, the country took almost twenty years to build itself once more into a strong military power.

The *Bismarck* was launched in Hamburg before the war began. The date was Valentine's Day 1939. The event was a major day for the Nazi German government. All the top Nazi officials—including Adolf Hitler himself—were present.

Dorothea von Loewenfeld came to Hamburg to christen the ship named after her grandfather. He was Otto von Bismarck, the so-called Iron Chancellor, who led Germany during the middle and latter parts

Adolf Hitler greets workers who built the
Bismarck in Hamburg on February 14, 1939,
the day of the ship's launching. Behind
him, second from right, is
Field Marshal Hermann Goering.

of the nineteenth century. Under Bismarck, Germany rose from a group of provinces to become a unified and powerful nation. Bismarck himself represented a kind of ruthless strength and determination. These were qualities that everyone thought the new ship should have.

In a speech at the launching ceremonies, Hitler asked that the ship's crew would be as strong as the ship and as strong as the person for whom the ship was being named.

At 823 feet (251 m), the ship was almost a sixth of a mile (a quarter of a kilometer) long. She was 120 feet (37 m) wide and weighed 42,000 tons. But in the official shipping records, the Germans lied about how much the ship weighed. After World War I, a treaty had been signed. This treaty said that no battleship could weigh more than 35,000 tons. Because of this, the Germans told the world that was how big the *Bismarck* was.

The *Bismarck* was well suited for battle. Her armament consisted of eight 15-inch (38-cm) guns. She also had twelve 5.9-inch (15-cm) guns and sixteen that were 4.1 inches (10.4 cm). The size of a gun refers to the diameter of the shells that can be fired from it. Not many other ships could release such large shells. The *Bismarck* also had six airplanes that could be launched from her deck by catapult.

The armor plating on the ship's sides was 13 inches (33 cm) thick. This would protect the ship from being damaged by enemy gunfire. The armor alone accounted for 16,000 tons of the ship's total weight.

Like the *Titanic* before her, the *Bismarck*'s hull was divided into separate compartments. In the unlikely event of an accident, the damaged compartments would fill up, but the water would stay in one section of the ship. Everyone thus thought the *Bismarck*, like the *Titanic*, was unsinkable.

On that Valentine's Day only the ship's hull, or main structure, was finished. The *Bismarck* slid into the water and was then towed to a dock. There it would be fitted out and completed. For months welders, electricians, and carpenters swarmed over the ship. They were adding all the final touches to complete the ship and make it ready for combat.

It wasn't until eighteen months after the launching that the *Bismarck* was ready to go to sea. On September 15, 1940, the ship sailed from Hamburg for sea trials. By then its crew had joined it. Recruits from the German navy came on board to staff the ship. It was wartime, and the average age of the sailors was twenty-one.

Despite performing reasonably well on the trials, there were some minor problems. These were not

The Bismarck, *at this point just
a hull, is launched.*

The Bismarck *being fitted out in Hamburg*

fully worked out until the following spring. In March 1941, the job was finally finished.

Then, during a new series of sea trials, the *Bismarck* reached a speed of 30 knots. A knot is slightly more than a land mile (1.6 km). A mile on land is 5,280 feet (1609 m). A mile at sea measures 6,076 feet (1852 m). This is known as a nautical mile.

During these trials, everything worked as planned and the ship was accepted and commissioned into the German navy. This long training period helped the crew to make the *Bismarck* a very well-run ship.

At the end of April the *Bismarck* would steam into the Atlantic to launch attacks on Allied ships. The ship would be joined by another German warship, the heavy cruiser *Prinz Eugen*. The Germans did not want to disturb anybody's warships. Their intention was to attack only merchant ships traveling in convoys. In this way supplies would be prevented from reaching Britain.

Hitler visited the battleship on May 5. In an elaborate speech he praised the *Bismarck* and its crew as "the pride of the Navy."

3

MEETING THE *HOOD*

By May 18, 1941, the *Bismarck* and *Prinz Eugen* were ready to sail from Gotenhafen, a port in the Baltic Sea. Because the Germans had seized Poland, they had given the city of Gdynia a German name. Supply ships would accompany the larger ships. These smaller ships would keep the big ships serviced with food, water, fuel, and ammunition for as long as needed. The ships' captains thought this would be about three months, time enough to disrupt British shipping.

The *Bismarck* and the *Prinz Eugen* sailed through the Baltic westward toward Norway. Eventually the ships would reach the unguarded Atlantic. Obviously, the ships' crews hoped no one would see them.

But the *Bismarck*'s captain sailed the big ship

The Bismarck (*left*) *is spotted from
the air in a Norwegian fjord in this photo
taken by a British Reconnaissance Unit group.*

The Bismarck (*background*), in a photo
in Norwegian waters taken from the Prinz Eugen.

through a narrow stretch of Norwegian water in broad daylight on May 21. The ships also arrived at and departed from Bergen, Norway, on that day. It was very easy for any local citizen to see the vessels. And this is exactly what happened. The ships were spotted and their directions were noted. A group from the British Reconnaissance Unit photographed the ships from the air. Soon officials in the British government knew the ships' locations.

Why the captain let the ship travel so close to land in daylight hours is just one of the many strange things about the *Bismarck*'s voyage.

Another mystery surrounds the *Bismarck*'s fuel supply. Before the ships left Norway the *Bismarck*'s captain should have made sure his ship had been refueled. But he didn't. It was essential that the ship leave for the open seas with as much fuel as possible. This factor became an important one as events later unfolded.

British intelligence experts thus found out where the German ships were and the British fleet came to life. It now became apparent that the British fleet would be sent out to track down—and destroy—the *Bismarck*.

At that time, most of the Royal Navy's ships were moored north of Scotland in the Orkney Islands, at a place called Scapa Flow. By midnight on May 21, two of the prize British ships, the *Hood* and the *Prince of Wales*, left Scapa. They were on their way to meet two smaller cruisers, the *Norfolk* and the *Suffolk*. British naval commanders assumed that all their ships would soon meet the *Bismarck*.

The *Bismarck* and the *Prinz Eugen* were steaming through the Arctic Ocean some 200 miles (320 km) northeast of Iceland. Then the *Bismarck* turned southwest into the Denmark Strait. The *Norfolk* and the *Suffolk* were waiting.

When the ships drew close, the *Bismarck* opened fire on the *Norfolk*, but visibility was bad because of fog. In 1941, radar was a relatively new invention. Often binoculars were the only way to trace another vessel, and good visibility was very important. There were no casualties and no major damage was done to the British ships. But radio reports were sent and received by other ships, and the *Hood* and the *Prince of Wales* were able to rush to the rescue.

The *Hood* was Great Britain's mightiest symbol of ocean supremacy. Between the two wars, the ship had been shown off around the world. The *Hood* was an even larger and more majestic ship than the *Bismarck*. Technically a battle cruiser, she was longer by about 30 feet (9 m). And because she could travel at 32 knots, the *Hood* was the fastest warship of her size.

The British battle cruiser Hood

The H.M.S. Norfolk *firing its guns during the engagement with the* Bismarck *in the Denmark Strait. The* Norfolk *and the* Suffolk *awaited the* Bismarck *and* Prinz Eugen *when they turned into the strait.*

But because the *Hood* was an older warship, her armor wasn't as strong. Some work had been done to strengthen the ship's sides, but her decks were still weak. The *Hood* was some twenty-five years old and the weapons of warfare had grown larger since she was built in 1916.

The *Hood* and the *Bismarck* had guns that were over 20 yards (18 m) long. These guns weighed 100 tons each. Now the two ships were steaming toward each other, bent on destruction. More than six thousand young British and German sailors waited for the confrontation.

And then it came. Within four minutes, the Germans on board the *Bismarck* fired five different times on the *Hood*. The *Hood* might have resisted these attacks, but one shell left its mark. This shell sped through the air and struck the *Hood's* unreinforced decks. The shell pierced the ship's deck and then went down into the heart of the ship.

A giant spout of flame shot out from the middle of the *Hood*. To some observers it was so high it seemed "to touch the sky." As the smoke began to clear, the same observers could see debris flying up through the air. The ship broke into two pieces and sank quickly.

Once the *Hood* was destroyed, the Germans turned to the *Prince of Wales*. The *Prince of Wales* was

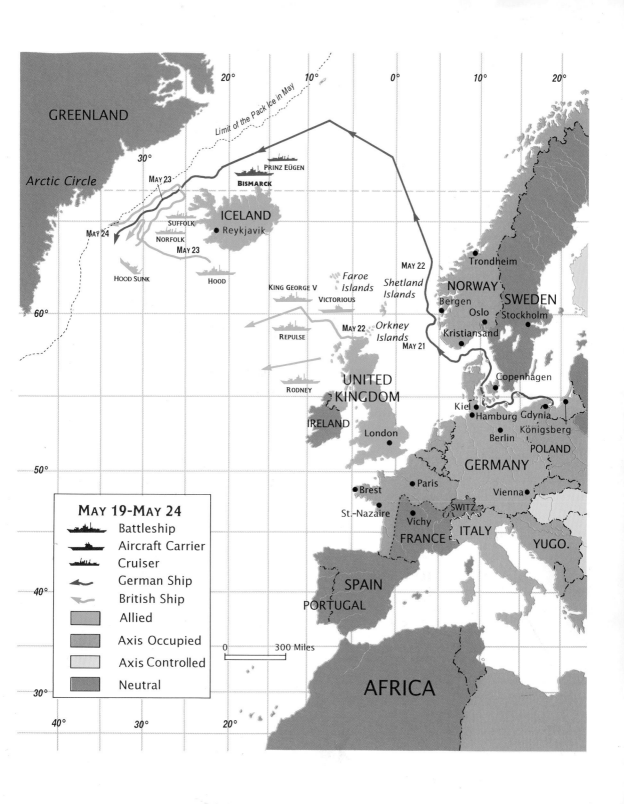

20°　10°　0°　10°　20°

GREENLAND

Limit of the Pack Ice in May

30°

Arctic Circle

MAY 23

MAY 24

PRINZ EÜGEN

BISMARCK

SUFFOLK
NORFOLK
MAY 23

ICELAND
● Reykjavik

HOOD SUNK

HOOD

Faroe Islands

Shetland Islands

MAY 22

Trondheim

KING GEORGE V

VICTORIOUS

Orkney Islands

MAY 22

MAY 22

MAY 21

NORWAY

Bergen
Oslo
Stockholm

SWEDEN

Kristiansand

REPULSE

60°

Copenhagen

UNITED
KINGDOM

RODNEY

IRELAND

London ●

Kiel
● Hamburg Gdynia
Königsberg
Berlin ●
POLAND

GERMANY

50°

● Brest
● Paris
Vienna ●

St.-Nazaire
Vichy ●
SWITZ.
ITALY
FRANCE
YUGO.

SPAIN

40°

PORTUGAL

30°

AFRICA

MAY 19–MAY 24

Battleship
Aircraft Carrier
Cruiser
German Ship
British Ship
Allied
Axis Occupied
Axis Controlled
Neutral

0　　300 Miles

40°　　30°　　20°

so close to the *Hood* that she had to make an abrupt turn to get out of the way. In a matter of only eleven minutes, the *Prince of Wales* had had enough. The ship had been hit by shells from both the *Bismarck* and the *Prinz Eugen*. One of the shells destroyed the *Prince of Wales*'s bridge, killing most of the sailors there.

Although the *Prince of Wales* fought back valiantly, the ship soon turned away and left the site. Like the *Bismarck*, the *Prince of Wales* was a new ship. But unlike the *Bismarck*, the British ship hadn't been broken in properly. There were lots of things that didn't work well. Everyone on board realized the *Prince of Wales* just wasn't strong enough to stand against the *Bismarck* alone.

When the battle was over only twenty minutes had gone by. The *Hood* had taken most of her crew with her to the bottom of the sea. Of fourteen hundred sailors, just three crew members from the *Hood* survived.

The British were horrified by what had happened to the mighty *Hood*. And they were angry. The *Hood* had been the symbol of British naval power. When news of the *Hood*'s sinking reached London, everyone was shocked and saddened. British morale was at an all-time low.

What the Germans hadn't counted on was that the *Prince of Wales* was a scrappy ship. Before she sailed off, the *Prince of Wales* had managed to do some damage to the *Bismarck*. Two shells had put holes in the side of the ship. The damage wasn't great, but the holes meant that salt water could flow in and mix with the ship's fuel supply. Suddenly the *Bismarck* had a serious problem.

The Bismarck *after being damaged by two shells from the* Prince of Wales. *The bow (right) sits lower in the water than the stern.*

The *Bismarck*'s crew realized what had happened. Some people think that at this point the Germans wanted to finish off their own wounded ship. The only other choice was to find a welcoming shipyard that would repair the damage to the *Bismarck*. Not only was the ship moving more slowly, but it was leaving a telltale trail of oil in the water as it steamed along.

And so, just hours after the *Bismarck* had scored a major naval victory for Germany, a decision was made: to head for the coast of France for repairs. The German commander of the *Bismarck* had ruled out a return to Germany for repairs. He was afraid that other British ships might catch the *Bismarck*. Hitler had greeted the news of the *Hood*'s sinking with joy. He would be very displeased to learn that the *Bismarck* was damaged.

Again on May 24, visibility was patchy all day. Fog came and went. Sometimes vision was fine. But at other times banks of fog made it almost impossible to see the nearby ships.

At some point on the evening of the twenty-fourth, when the visibility was all right, the *Bismarck* sighted the *Suffolk*. The British cruiser was still shadowing the *Bismarck*. The German ship fired shells at the British cruiser. It now seems that this was a tactic designed to divert British attention. While this happened, the *Prinz Eugen* slipped quietly out of the battle zone and made her way safely to the French coast.

At 3 A.M. on May 25, the British *Suffolk* lost sight of the *Bismarck*. Over thirty hours of shadowing the great ship were over. The *Bismarck* had tried a ploy. For a period of hours, the Germans followed a zigzag course. This method was often used to lose a pursuing ship. The British were baffled. It appears that the *Suffolk* lost track of the *Bismarck* when it was making just such a maneuver.

Determined to relocate the battleship, the British assumed, rightly, that the *Bismarck* was heading for the safety of occupied France. They reasoned that as the ship got closer to the French coast, it would get protection from the German air force, the Luftwaffe.

The British naval commanders thought that the only way they could destroy the *Bismarck* was by air. Pilots in a Catalina amphibian aircraft finally located the *Bismarck* again. Then it was time to launch an air attack on the battleship. But visibility made taking off and landing on an aircraft carrier difficult. And it would make finding the target a hard task as well.

The aircraft carrier *Victorious* stood by, ready to launch the planes that would drop torpedoes on the *Bismarck*. The planes were primitive by today's standards. They were called Swordfish biplanes and traveled at a very slow 95 miles (152 km) per hour. They were to be launched from the deck of the *Victorious* and sent off in pursuit of the *Bismarck*. Each carried a crew of three: a pilot, an observer, and a gunner. Their ammunition consisted of a single torpedo, strapped to the plane's belly.

And so they headed toward the *Bismarck*. It was the first time in history that a battleship at sea was to be attacked by planes launched from a carrier.

Again visibility was uneven. As soon as the *Bismarck* realized she was being attacked from the air, she resumed her zigzag course. This made targeting the ship very difficult, particularly from such unsophisticated aircraft and in such poor weather.

The Swordfish planes first mistook a U.S. Coast Guard cutter for the *Bismarck*. But the pilots realized their error just in time. When they finally found the *Bismarck*, they managed to send one torpedo to the ship, but it didn't do any damage. Then the planes had to make their way back to the *Victorious* through great banks of fog. They had to land their craft on the deck of the ship in dangerously high seas.

The crew members on board the *Bismarck* finally realized that once again they needed to alter their course. They knew they had to confuse their chasers. The most important thing was to get away from the cruisers and small craft that were dogging their progress. More than anything else the Germans needed to get their ship to the French coast for refueling and repairs.

Then through a trick of fate—and nothing else— the British lost sight of the *Bismarck*. For nearly thirty hours, not one of the Royal Navy's ships that had been tracking her had any notion of the *Bismarck*'s whereabouts. The *Suffolk*, especially, had been keeping a close watch on the ship. Suddenly on May 25 the *Bismarck* vanished, as if she had never existed.

Of course, the *Bismarck* hadn't really disappeared. The ship had merely shaken off her pursuers —for a while. The weather was largely responsible for this. Patches of dense fog came and went. And as the *Bismarck* zigzagged she disappeared from the *Suffolk*'s radar screen.

The *Bismarck*'s crew was buying time. They even began to build a dummy smokestack. They thought that if they could construct another funnel—this one made of wood—and install it on the ship's superstructure, they could fool the enemy into thinking the *Bismarck* was another ship! But the rough seas kept them from finishing the project, and the idea was abandoned.

All through the day on May 25 the seas became rougher and rougher. Trying to find the ship became harder and harder. Finally, a British reconnaissance plane sighted the battleship. The more time passed, the closer the *Bismarck* would be to the coast of France and safety. By this time, all the British ships in the area were running low on fuel. Also, these ships were small and not very well armed. They simply were not equipped to fight something as large as the *Bismarck*.

It seemed that the only chance left was another air attack. The British aircraft carrier *Ark Royal* was

A Swordfish biplane. These planes, based on aircraft carriers, made torpedo attacks on the Bismarck.

ordered into action to provide planes for a second airborne strike on the *Bismarck*.

At dawn on May 26, fifteen tiny Swordfish planes were readied for takeoff. The sea was extremely rough and the winds were almost of hurricane force. Reports indicate that the *Ark Royal* rose as much as 55 feet (17 m) in the churning water. By midday the planes were ready to take off.

By one of those cruel twists that seem to happen a lot in wartime, the pilots mistook their own cruiser, the *Sheffield*, for the *Bismarck*. The plane crews were merely told that any ship they found near the position given them would be the enemy. The *Bismarck* had one funnel and the *Sheffield* had two. So it was a strange mistake to make. But it happened. The planes fired torpedoes at the wrong ship!

And the blunder grew even more bizarre. The torpedoes had been improperly timed and launched. Most of them detonated on contact with the water rather than with the metal hull of their target. The *Sheffield* was spared any damage and was safe. The planes then returned to the *Ark Royal* to prepare themselves for a strike against the correct target.

By 7:00 on the evening of May 26, the crew of the *Bismarck* had begun to feel confident. They hadn't been found. In two hours it would be dark and then they would be safe, at least until morning. For all the ships, however, both British and German, fuel supplies were starting to get dangerously low. Because of low fuel—and damage, too—almost all the vessels were forced to reduce their speeds drastically.

The confidence on board the *Bismarck*, however, was short-lived. At 8:54 that evening, the squadron of the Swordfish planes from the *Ark Royal* spotted the *Bismarck*. The seas were getting rougher and now there were rain squalls to add to the visibility problem.

In fact, the weather was so bad that the pilots were not exactly sure if they had hit their target. When the planes returned to the *Ark Royal,* their crews talked of at least one torpedo strike to the middle of the *Bismarck.* There was also the possibility that another had hit the stern of the ship. But no one could be completely sure.

Oddly enough, German U-boat *U 556* had spotted the *Ark Royal* just as the planes were about to leave the carrier to attack the *Bismarck.* The U-boat's captain put his periscope up. There, almost directly above his submerged submarine, was the *Ark Royal.* With the carrier in perfect sight, the captain had to face a sad fact: He had no torpedoes left with which to sink the *Ark Royal.* If there had been torpedoes left, the *Bismarck* might have been saved. And, almost certainly, the *Ark Royal* would have gone to the bottom of the sea.

The *Sheffield* had come so close to the *Bismarck* that crew members could see flames and smoke billowing from the German ship.

One British pilot noticed as his plane was returning to the *Ark Royal* that the *Bismarck* seemed to turn in two great circles and then come to a complete halt in the ocean. Some observers concluded that the ship's rudder and/or propellers had been hit. The

Bismarck seemed able to steer in only one direction. Could this mean the great ship was unable to maneuver?

In fact, it turned out that the *Bismarck's* rudder structure had been damaged. This was caused by a torpedo that had struck the side of the ship. The propellers were all right. There was a slight chance that the rudder might be repaired, but it would be a suicide mission for divers who would have to be lowered from the side of the ship into turbulent waters. Explosive blasts would be needed to unjam the mechanism and they might damage the unharmed propellers. The *Bismarck's* steering compartment had also been hit, so the ship's problems were doubly serious.

With the final strike only hours away, all British ships in the vicinity began to converge on the scene. A convoy of five small destroyers even drew near to surround the pride of the German navy. It seemed as if the *Bismarck* was a sitting duck.

7

THE BISMARCK IS SUNK (MAY 27)

By 11:00 P.M. on May 26, the *Bismarck* was surrounded by British destroyers, battleships, and cruisers. In an attempt to get the ship's log back to Germany, the crew on the *Bismarck* tried to launch one of the battleship's airplanes. But the catapult system failed and the airplane had to be dumped into the sea. It was feared that the plane's fuel tanks might explode if the ship was struck again.

There were flattering—and morale-boosting—radio messages from Hitler praising the crew. But most of the people on board the *Bismarck* sensed the heroics were false. They all seemed to realize that the end was near.

By dawn on May 27 it was raining and the seas were rougher than ever. The British ships had so little

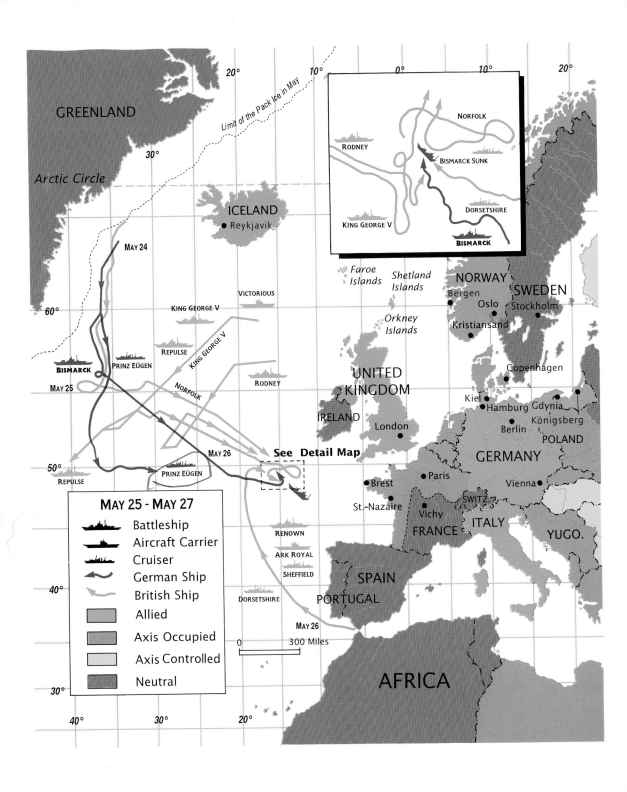

GREENLAND

Arctic Circle

Limit of the Pack Ice in May

ICELAND
• Reykjavik

MAY 24

BISMARCK

PRINZ EÜGEN

MAY 25

REPULSE

KING GEORGE V

REPULSE

VICTORIOUS

KING GEORGE V

NORFOLK

RODNEY

MAY 26

PRINZ EÜGEN

REPULSE

See Detail Map

Faroe
Islands

Shetland
Islands

Orkney
Islands

NORWAY

SWEDEN

Bergen

Oslo

Stockholm

Kristiansand

Copenhagen

UNITED
KINGDOM

Kiel

Hamburg Gdynia

IRELAND

London

Berlin

Königsberg

POLAND

GERMANY

Brest

Paris

Vienna

St.-Nazaire

Vichy

SWITZ.

ITALY

YUGO.

RENOWN

ARK ROYAL

SHEFFIELD

FRANCE

SPAIN

PORTUGAL

DORSETSHIRE

MAY 26

AFRICA

Detail map (inset):

NORFOLK

RODNEY

BISMARCK SUNK

DORSETSHIRE

KING GEORGE V

BISMARCK

Legend:

MAY 25 - MAY 27

Battleship
Aircraft Carrier
Cruiser
German Ship
British Ship
Allied
Axis Occupied
Axis Controlled
Neutral

0   300 Miles

fuel that a target time of 10:00 A.M. was set. If the *Bismarck* wasn't sunk by that hour, the ships would have to turn, leave the vicinity, and head back to England. Without fuel, they too would be sitting ducks.

The British cruiser *Rodney* joined the fray and began the final assault at 8:43 A.M. Smoke came from the *Rodney*'s guns as they launched a final attack on the *Bismarck*. The *King George V* joined in, followed by the *Norfolk* and *Dorsetshire*. The doomed *Bismarck* refused to give up. In fact, she retaliated desperately, and sent a few well-aimed shells toward the British ships. One of these hit the *Rodney* and damaged one of the torpedo-launching tubes.

But time was running out for the *Bismarck*. Shells from the British ships hit the *Bismarck*'s bridge and affected that ship's firing accuracy. Less than an hour later, the British could see flames shooting all around the ship through holes in its side. But they could also see the German flag still flying. The ship refused to surrender.

The fuel situation was getting desperate, and the battle was almost over. An order was given to fire two last torpedoes. The only ship with torpedoes left was the *Dorsetshire*. These hit the *Bismarck* and dealt the final blows.

Left: a crew member of the H.M.S. Dorsetshire,
the British cruiser that dealt the final blows.
Above: sailors on the Dorsetshire display
an 8-inch shell of the type
fired at the Bismarck.

At 10:40 A.M. the *Bismarck* turned over and sank. She went down stern first and bow last. Of the 2,400 crew on board, only about 115 survived in the oily, stormy waters. The *Dorsetshire* stayed behind, willing to pick up any survivors. But again, fate dealt a cruel blow to the men of the *Bismarck*. The *Dorsetshire* picked up a signal that U-boats were nearby. So, in the midst of rescue operations, the *Dorsetshire* had to scurry away to safety.

The glorious ship came to a woeful end only nine days after leaving on her first mission. But it had taken 8 battleships and battle cruisers, 2 aircraft carriers, 4 heavy cruisers, 7 light cruisers, 21 destroyers, and 6 submarines to do the job.

On May 27, 1941, only hours after the battle, English prime minister Winston Churchill stood up to make a speech in the House of Commons. When he began, Churchill knew only that his navy was battling the *Bismarck*. But before the session was over, he was

Surviving crew members of the Bismarck *being picked up by the* Dorsetshire. *In the end, only 115 out of about 2,400 crew members survived.*

handed a definite message: The *Bismarck* had been sunk. And the *Hood* had been avenged.

And so a vital turning point occurred in World War II. Never again would a German fleet venture so far out into the Atlantic. And never again would the German navy have as much strength.

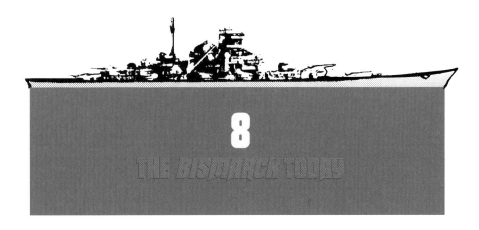

8
THE *BISMARCK* TODAY

And there the great ship still lies today, buried under almost 16,000 feet (5 km) of chilly Atlantic waters. Considering the number of shells that struck the *Bismarck*, the sunken ship is in surprisingly good condition. The ship sits, almost upright, on the bottom of the ocean. Since witnesses who saw the *Bismarck* go down say it turned over completely before it sank, it may have turned over several more times on its way down to the bottom of the Atlantic.

On June 8, 1989, 600 miles (960 km) off the coast of the French port of Brest, the *Bismarck* was found. The mission had begun the summer before but had not been successful. Now nine days and more than two hundred hours of searching had provided the sunken treasure.

51

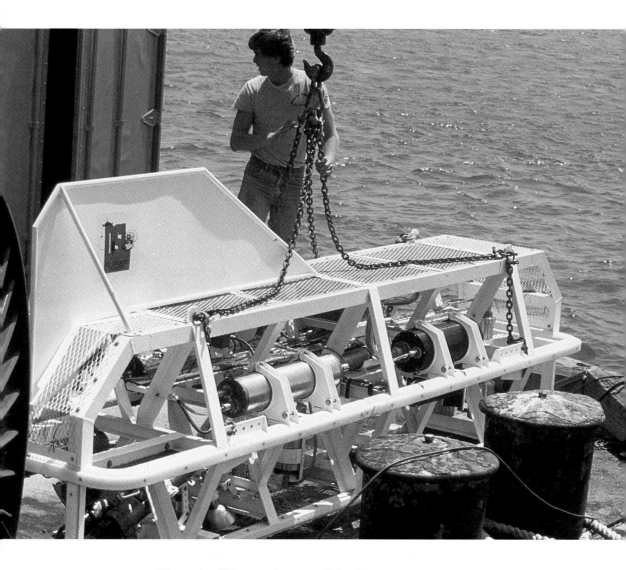

The sledlike submersible Argo *was sent to the bottom of the Atlantic to take video and still images of the* Bismarck.

The search for the *Bismarck* was given impetus by Dr. Robert Ballard from the Woods Hole Oceanographic Institution in Massachusetts. The expedition was funded jointly by the National Geographic Society, Turner Broadcasting, and a private group of investors known as the Quest Group Ltd.

The *Bismarck* is more or less where everyone thought it would be. Ballard is keeping the exact location of the ship secret from everybody except the German people. They will then be able to decide if they want to raise the remains of the battleship. Under the laws of the sea, the ship belongs to Germany.

Modern science provided the technology for finding the *Bismarck*. Sonar allowed the scientists to scan the ocean bottom. Sonar also helped them realize that this part of the Atlantic was anything but flat. Instead, it is crossed by a series of undersea "mountains" of rock.

Most of these discoveries were made by the *Argo*, a small submersible. The sonar equipment was carried on this sledlike submersible, which Ballard and his scientists had used to explore the *Titanic* in the summer of 1985.

Each day the supply ship on the ocean's surface, *Star Hercules*, would release the *Argo* to the ocean bottom. A one-inch-thick cable was the only thing connecting *Argo* to the surface. It took almost two

The wood planking of the Bismarck's deck
remains remarkably well preserved after
half a century below the ocean.

hours for the submersible to get down the 3 miles (4.8 km) to the ocean floor. The rough terrain made it difficult for the *Argo* to get around.

There were video and still cameras on board the *Argo*. These allowed photographic images to be made of any objects sighted. The *Argo* then sent these images up to TV monitors in the surface vessel. There the researchers remained, their eyes glued to the TV screens.

The pictures relayed by the *Argo* are fascinating. They reveal that the *Bismarck* is missing much of its superstructure. The forward bridge and the conning tower remain. But the ship's single funnel is gone. Some of the *Bismarck's* stern had broken away from the rest of the hull.

Some of the ship's guns seem to have broken off, too. The four main turret guns are gone, but all others remain. This probably happened as the ship sank farther and farther to the bottom. Water pressure would have caused the gun mountings to snap. Some of the teak decking is untouched, even by fifty years of the sea. Ballard suggests that the Germans may have scuttled the ship themselves. To scuttle means to open the ship up to let water in slowly. This lets the ship settle gently on the bottom. This, says Ballard, rather than the holes in the ship's side from torpedoes, may be the reason the ship sank in 1941. Scuttling would also have kept the state-of-the-art ship from falling into enemy hands.

But wouldn't the Germans have scuttled the ship much sooner? As soon as the rudder was damaged, most of the crew knew the ship was finished. Wouldn't they have scuttled the ship then and there? They might also have managed to save most of the crew. Why wait until the ship was virtually ablaze? And why wait until there was almost no chance of saving many lives?

Ballard found the *Bismarck* in excellent condition —astonishing when you consider that the British had poured more than three hundred shells and torpedoes into the *Bismarck* in an effort to sink her. And there are also those swastikas, grim reminders of a black period in world history.

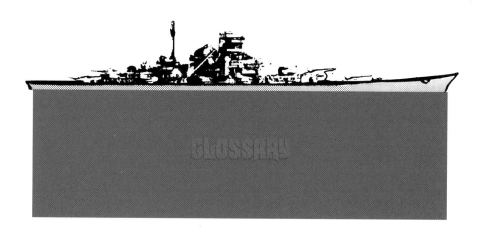

GLOSSARY

Aircraft carrier—A ship having a flat deck that is used by airplanes as a landing field at sea

Battle cruiser—A class of warship that is almost as large and powerful as a battleship but whose armor is not as strong as a battleship

Battleship—A class of warship, one that is the most heavily armed and protected

Bow—The front, usually pointed, end of a ship

Bridge—A platform, above the top deck, near the front of a ship, where the captain is stationed. All navigation is done from the bridge.

Cruiser—A middle-sized warship, larger than a destroyer but smaller than a battleship or battle cruiser

57

Destroyer—A small but fast warship with some guns and strike equipment; also used as protection for larger, slower ships

Hull—The bottom part of a ship, including the sides, bow, and stern

Keel—A plate on the bottom of a ship's hull

Knot—A sea mile. Because a nautical mile is 6,076 feet (1,852 m), instead of 5,280 feet (1,609 m), a knot is slightly more than a land mile. A ship's speed is traditionally measured in knots.

Log—A written record of a ship's activities

Nautical mile—A measure at sea of 6,076 feet (1,852 m)

Propeller—A device made up of a series of revolving blades that drives a ship

Rudder—A large, flat piece of metal used for steering. It is mounted on the stern of a ship.

Stern—The rear end of a ship. It is usually squared off or slightly rounded.

Superstructure—The upper part of a ship, above the hull

U-boat—A German submarine. The word is short for *Unterseeboot.*

FINDING OUT MORE
ABOUT THE *BISMARCK*

There are only a few books for young readers that tell about the *Bismarck*. One of them is by William L. Shirer, and it is called *The Sinking of the Bismarck*. It was published by Random House in their Landmark series in 1962. An adult book, but a good one—and a short one—to read is by C. S. Forester. It is called *The Last Nine Days of the Bismarck* and was published in Boston in 1955 by Little, Brown. It does invent dialogue, but with great skill.

More detailed information is given in two well-known books about the incident. The more recent, by Ludovic Kennedy, is called *Pursuit: The Chase and Sinking of the Bismarck*. It was published in New York by The Viking Press in 1974. Older—and harder to find—is a book by Russell Grenfell. It is called *The Bismarck Episode*, and was published in New York by Macmillan in 1949.

The story of the *Bismarck* also forms part of many larger books that tell about World War II. One of the most interesting—and readable—is found in *The Grand Alliance*, the third volume of Winston Churchill's *The Second World War*. This was first published in the United States in 1950 in Boston by Houghton Mifflin.

More recently, The National Geographic Society has released a videotape of the 1989 Ballard expedition, which includes interviews with *Bismarck* survivors as well as up-to-date photos of the sunken ship as it remains today.

For fun, there's also a full-length film, *Sink the Bismarck!* (1960). Although it contains a fictitious love story, there are also good restaged battle scenes, which seem to be accurate. There is also wonderful newsreel footage at the beginning that shows the actual launching of the *Bismarck*. It is extremely interesting to see how a big ship is launched and also to catch a glimpse of how the Nazis put on a big show.

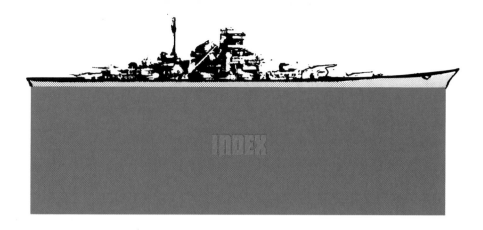

INDEX

ABOUT
THE AUTHOR

Frank Sloan has worked as an art director, editor, and author during his long and varied career in children's book publishing. Of his previous book, *Titanic*, the *Book Report* said "Sloan has done an excellent job of presenting the facts without sentimentalizing the tragedy," and ALA *Booklist* called it "a highly readable account." Frank Sloan is a board member of both the Children's Book Council and the Society of Children's Book Writers. He divides his time between New York City and upstate New York.